Where Will I Find *America?*

Where Will I Find *America*?

TAMER SAID MOSTAFA

(He, Him, His)

Copyright © 2021 by Tamer Said Mostafa

All rights reserved. No part of this book may be reproduced or used in any manner without written permission of the copyright owner except for the use of quotations in a book review.

ISBN: 978-0-9720626-0-2

"We do not know enough about the mind,
   or how the conundrum of the imagination
dictates, discovers,
or can dismember what we feel,
   or what we find.

Perhaps
one must learn to trust
one's terror"

   —from James Baldwin's *Jimmy's Blues and Other Poems*

after Malcolm X's speech at the Embassy in Los Angeles (1961)

hold your applause for the end if it doesn't disorient
you more than the napalm you praise
let this be for you as it is for the unnamed
the ancestors restore luminaries from their gilded
casts of gold lost to the cosmos
his grandmother's backyard is seen from a red light
in Meadowview
two carbon barrel side arms radiate the night until it
immortally resembles march
the martyr's homage is a stone's throw
to & from the margins
stones are a homeland's oxymoron of mortar
& mirrors
eulogies are epics until they drip
from a rope-strung tree & become lotuses
there is always an again & an again

                                                            praise
                        be for
        the ancestors

                                seen
                                  in
                                the night
                                            march

                        to   the
                land's
                                            mirrors
                                        until they
                                        become   us
                                                    again

_____

Contents

After Malcolm X's Speech at the Embassy in Los Angeles (1961)

I.

The Night Bone Thugs-n-Harmony Reunited 3
Savior 5
Prayer as a Time-Lapse for the Procrastinator 6
A Childhood Around 1999 8
the coming fire 9
Tweaking 10
Shame 11
Rite of Passage 12
There is No Blood 13
Lamb Slaughter 14
Learning Arabic in Adulthood 15
Letter to Lucy Corin 16
2011: On the Metro to Tahrir 17
Before Janaza Prayer 18
A Panegyric for a Self, Hidden Within 20
Composition 21
I Am Afraid of Living 23
of Valley and Desert 24
On Having Children 26
Transformation 28

II.

When Bone Thugs-n-Harmony Outshined Phil Collins on His Own Song 31

The Mind is a Milk Curdle 32
Poem at Ten 33
The City 35
McGaw Street 37
Post-mortem 39
Eating a Peach on the Drive to Porterville 40
"Slow down before you end up in the water like the rest of them!" 41
Midnight in South Lake Tahoe 43
Us in the kitchen, listening to Maxwell's "Pretty Wings" 44
Dameron Hospital, Stockton 46
Getting Dunked on by Jacki Gemelos 48
Mourning Diana Solaegui in Solitude 49
Elegies for the Central Valley 50
I Lip-synced Ready for the World Instead of Pushing Carts for Target 55
In Defense of *Queef* 57
Brookside Park Blacktop 59
A Robin Stopped by This Morning 60
In South Sacramento 62
The Valley, as Told from a Pet Hospital Parking Lot 63
stockton 65
Kayaking off Brannan Island 68
After I Returned 69
To the Passerby 70

III.

"Days of Our Livez" is a better Bone Thugs-n-Harmony song than "Tha Crossroads" 73
Failed Migration to Egypt, 2007 74
from **trilateral roots** 76

My Grandmother Would Have Loved
    Chick-fil-A **77**
To Make Love in a Hearse **79**
The Origin of Fear **80**
I Haven't Been Keeping Up on Pluto Much These
    Days **81**
Existential Crisis through the Windstorm, in a
    Humboldt County Yurt **83**
The Poet's Partner Karaokes "Rainbow" by
    Kesha **84**
Ascent **85**
Inauguration Day, 2017 **86**
I Must Have Been Beautiful *aka Shyla Styles Has
    Died* **87**
The Sunflower **89**
All I Know is How to Stop Breathing **91**
Listening to *Man on the Moon: The End of Day* **92**
Fatima's Martydom **94**
Nabra's Moon **96**
Where Will I Find *America?* **98**
Reclamation **99**

Acknowledgements 101
About the Author 109

I.

"Our people carry the homeland in their souls. You can go wherever you want, but you'll always have it in your heart," —Baba

"That's such a heavy thing to carry," —Nidali

—from Randa Jarrar's *A Map of Home*

The Night Bone Thugs-n-Harmony Reunited

My father is a learned magician,
morphing fingers through the flesh of his stomach
to wish that the seamed scar would fish out
decades-old nine-millimeter fragments
layered short like staccato notes.
He traces their origins,
fleeing from the park named after victory.
His hands blister,
depleted and dripping with red wax
before disappearing in a smoke snap
and he tucks the city's secrets with him,
a double-edged sword
suctioned through his nose
because the conundrum of bullet wounds
is that they are still prone
like a mandolin's sound hole
busied by bronze strings,
ordering their beginnings
be remedied, or at least
reconsidered to nothingness.
I ask the city for my father's return,
stow his picture to each passerby
ignoring the vortex of its history,
a needle slipping from vinyl.
The year on back is '88,
he blesses the foam from a forty ounce,
belly-dances the concrete to survival
with a broom stick
buffed with steam and blood,
a keffiyeh tied at the waist
spinning like an inferno.

And I tell myself
that the music must be true
to keep his magic for this long.

Savior

Four years passed since I failed to save
my mother from drowning. The water transformed
into ice once she fell through the surface.
I still jumped.
I stabbed the ice with a steak knife
until I collapsed, surrounded by frozen shavings
above her body.

Pop's callused fists could have shattered
the ice, but they just sat on his knees.
One pinching a cigarette,
the other gripping his belt
smeared with blood.

There wasn't time to cry.
I had to cook his food,
pick up his medication,
and tuck him in with the remote
and a cold Budweiser.

The other day I tripped
over the broken skateboard
he bashed across my back.
My mother helped me up,
wiped the blood from my forehead,
kissed my swollen cheek.

Prayer as a Time-Lapse for the Procrastinator

The *adhan* commences obedience upon a dream
that supersedes me   when I am alone.

The past empties its transgressions
for prayer to interrupt sleep like a foreteller

of the perils to come.

There, you are the morning's *mu'adhin*
an index finger dispersed in each ear

swaying your body   side to side

to tempt the chain of the world
into renouncing mortality.

The *zebibah* on your forehead
is still wet from washing   its blessings
migrate the push and pull of an odyssey's dawning

reduced to odds and ends.

Stand feet to feet   and shoulder to shoulder
against the tug of forgetfulness

desperate to split the precision.

A hand-stitched mat is our canvas to shepherd
worship through this juncture of time
that cannot exist if we do not name it.

Allahu Akbar

I invoke our demons upon opposite palms
suppressed atop my chest   with enough speed
to reconcile the future's thoughts and mythos.

Allahu Akbar

(you repeat after me)

in a compulsion
that urges the angels to salvage our origins
amongst the universe's myriad of corridors.

The journey is as much a fable
of how I began as a clot of blood between your ribs
and backbone

in this land distempered like a labyrinth.
We bow for ruku'.   I   an atlas of latitudes.

You   the hand   and the ink,

that keeps me synchronous
encircling the paralysis.

A Childhood Around 1999

Sometimes playing basketball in the slanted driveway.
A white plastic file crate with the bottom sawed out,
nailed off-center between the roof and garage.

After rain, I used chalk from my mother's office
to retrace the free-throw line, three-point line,
and other spots washed to the sidewalk.

The out of bounds areas were marked on the left
by the untrimmed red cedars wrapped in webs
and the plot of bark separating walkway
from driveway on the right.

And the street too, when the ball rolled
to the opposite gutter,
the neighbors not honking to say hello,
peddlers on bikes who picked pre-rotting fruit
from the ground.

Local older kids who walked in cliques at night
tore the crate from its dirt outline on the gray paint,
left it next to the erect nails on the cement.

My mother, going door to door,
polite as a bible saleswoman
asking for answers and coming back with nothing
from both sides of every duplex down the way.

My father, standing on his truck bed
with the crate and a nail gun clenched in one hand,
turning to the street after shooting each nail.

the coming fire

each night we see
a shifting flicker
in a house
down the street

the owner traverses
his rooms
lugging butane
and cleaning bleach
in a biohazard waste bin

the blinds are down
but he knows
that we know
he's a chef
working silent
as a conifer's sway

and the next dawn
he ponders sleep
after a prolonged absence
strikes a matchstick
to a cigarette

the new warmth
catching
the thin layers
of sheet rock

Tweaking

I am alone in a parked car
near a convenience store
looking for a fix the size of a mustard seed.
I scratch my neck and forehead
where the sweat covers my eyes,
like the time I swam in a lake
to find a fishing rod that dropped out of the boat.

I remember the murkiness,
how the water flushed
my body's weight to the bottom,
and the mud enveloping
my feet that continued to sink
into the sharp white shells
catching each toe
when I started flutter kicking
towards the surface.

Upon returning to shore without the rod,
my grandmother, hearing of my expedition,
scolded me of the diseases in the water
that would make me sick beyond repair,
and I watched her catch a catfish
with a strand of line strung
to a stick on one end,
and a hook on the other.

It's the middle of the night
and I scour the floorboards,
scratching the fibers of the carpet
underneath my fingernails.
I need to keep looking.

Shame

1
The father and his teenage son are moving an oval shaped coffee table and its glass top from the garage to the living room. They don't speak until the father counts. On three they lift the table   facing each other   the father backpedaling. The son   underestimating the table's weight drops his left hand and the table wobbles   the glass top sliding to the edge. He catches it in time with his free hand   glimpses up to his father staring   standing straight   both hands steady under the table.

2
The father and his adult son are moving a three-seat brown couch with cushions attached   from a truck to the new house. They speak   making sure neither loses grip when they lift it a few feet above the ground. Facing each other   they focus on the white trimmed door frame   the father shuffling back towards the entryway   twisting the couch. The father   forgetting the closet's gold doorknob orders the son to push and when it happens   his hand catches in the gap between the knob and the couch's wood frame. The father stops his movement   grimaces   shuts his eyes to the direction of his son who still holds his end.

Rite of Passage

They called me sand ▮▮▮
the schoolyard bullies who
droned like mosquitoes do
on a swamp in summer's heat.

There was a beauty to it
the bruised eye and cracked ribs
that echoed in the oak wood
mirror frame.

My father scraped the mudded blood
off with a washcloth he used for
changing oil. My face chafed,
matching his beaten leather jacket.

He took me outside   lit a cigar
and sent me back to school
with an extra set of keys
cusped between my knuckles.

It was my third week of 7th grade
in September   2001.

There is No Blood

There is no blood
on the black and white
pawed pit bull
that lies in the gutter
its only movements
inflicted by the wind.

The owner hurries
like he's never hurried before
to resuscitate it on the front lawn.
He puts his hands
on the dog's chest
massaging the muscles
trying to invigorate
a kind of spark.

He cries a potent cry
hoping to add a touch
of robustness to the tongue
that hangs to the side
and the dry ears
he strokes for comfort.

After composing himself
he retreats inside
for a black garbage bag
ripped at the seams
drawstring draped
around his hand.

It is overcast and raining
but there is no blood.

Lamb Slaughter

A man with soggy Egyptian currency, and a son,
walks to the kofta stand,
a 10-inch butcher knife pitched on a register.
At eighteen, the son sits,
begging to witness the authentic method.
It happens outside on marble tile,
where flies nibble at crusted grout.
The man winks, recites an Arabic blessing,
the son translating every second or third word.
He studies his father's swing,
two hands and with elbows pointed out,
a brief lull. After blood sifts
past the metal grate onto the base
of his Converse sneakers
and the head stops purging the marble,
the son tries to solve
each crack in the tile.
Careful not to slip, he squats next to
the butcher who clips a slit in the hind leg,
curls his lips, and inflates the carcass
to peel the coat off with a filet knife.
The man hollers for another limping lamb,
pinches the knife with his shirt,
hands it to the son.

Learning Arabic in Adulthood

Tropes collapse upon one another
by beginning with their endings in sight.

Language is the continuum a carousel
distorts into formlessness   and futility.

Moments before your Oldsmobile dashboard
whittles the swelter of summer into zealousness
you whisper

Aziza [عزيزة] *Aziza* [عزيزة] *Aziza* [عزيزة]

liberating it's   *Taa Marbuta*
from becoming dormant on someone else's threshold.

Here lies the freezeframes sanctioned
amidst the miscarriage of memory.

I take your labor   unfulfilled like a stalemate
and begin the painful work of speaking.

Letter to Lucy Corin

—after Joe Wenderoth

When I was younger
I remember
hearing
about xenophobia
(and I've understood since the attacks
that xenophobia is just

twisting
a pressure valve)

and I remember conditioning
myself
to absorb the abuse
as some form of pity
to see the treatment
as proof of my existence
a recessive nerve
captivated by pain.

Today, I sit in the car
next to my father's dark brown skin.
I listen to his accent
mercifully trying to dissolve
into another language
he will never master.
How thick
how hard to understand.

And I remember you.

2011: On the Metro to Tahrir

When the church blew to rubble and rebar
we left Alexandria in an enigma because gravity
was a renegade,
that if these walls couldn't stall the exodus
of picture frames braided with wire and d-rings to tile,
what can we ask of cadavers thrashed through craters
like a wonder's ruins riddled to the seabed?

My father says it starts with an awakening,
his father bringing him to *al-Muqattam* mountain
to see Cairo's composite buried like voices
under the city's mosques, mustered into aftermath.
Their legacy is as lasting as millstones,
and the true stories are never wounded.

A man on the aisle tethers prayer beads
between his thumb and forefinger
                                  praise glory & greatness
for each powder blue bead sliding the twine
until tallying all ninety-nine.
He is their hydrangea
strumming from an amber jellabiya
like sheepskin.
He commissions
his eldered hands into mine
so I can feel him hunger
for the cypress noosed with bull's-eyes
for his garland swallowed by the river
for the corpse that will sing to generations
through the mud.

Before Janaza Prayer

—at a cemetery in Helwan

I complain to the nameplate
that its Arabic is not strung together
with any short vowels
converging their memorization on end.

Somehow, I interpret
the Japanese Garden in the distance
carrying *Umm Kulthum* away from a congregation
as she delivers her eulogy.

We were back in America
when *Baba* cupped his palms with one swoop
dipped them in a hypothetical bucket
of well-water on the ground
and mimicked circular movements
from his head down.
This is how you wash the body   he said.

A gold ring   engraved with the name for god
stifles my finger   I stick the crook
of my pinky nail
into the calligraphy of a matronymic
missing from the sandstone   *this was once yours*   I say
this was from gedati   endeavoring her breath
for mortality to travel across land
and ocean like a solstice.

It is now my time to return home
but *Baba* will stay   flying his twenty-foot kite
amongst the vista.

And when the skyline's juncture
severs the cotton string from anchor,
he will idolize the magnitude
of climbing each rooftop,
searching for its corpse.

A Panegyric for a Self, Hidden Within

I journeyed the trail of its being
like the oxidized imprint
of Nefertiti's tapered headdress
flaring atop a copper plate.
A wide *jellabiya* and tight *kufi*
sheltered the bafflement of my body,
its siphoning an Arabic accent,
the rising intonation of a longing
translated to a melodic madness.

I arrived, believing the existence
would leap from a limestone's surface
and ingurgitate me in a whirl
of humid sand tumbling from an apex,
or reorient me within the waters
lucent under the Citadel,
until what emerged was a spirit
immersed in a secluded history
and a lone quest concluded.

I returned over the original route,
confronting the figures of my steps
doused in the analogy of stallions,
forelocks hoarding the formula
of virtue, weather-beaten and looted.
It was then that I visualized
the presence, interned inward
like a land of walled bondmen
hurling rubble at the blockade.

Composition

—for my father and after *Purple Rain*

We have finished prayer
upon that rare desert rain
its purple current
skating the shutters
and velvet prayer rugs.

I use my fingers
to supplicate
for the America
I'll return to
for the idyll of Egypt
that will linger
interred under sugarcane.

You sit next to me
with one hand
sunk on my back
like the strap of a guitar
weighted with wounds
the other letting a cigarette
shrivel to dust.

I hear the roots
of my name
spinning like a wet towel
to conquer the smoke
to lead the matter
from the fibers
of an oak grain.

You direct your body
towards the *Qibla*
whispering to God

*here is the part of me
I give to the world.*

I Am Afraid of Living

Laying in a damp bed
next to a purifier circulating
the air for particles to trap
I stay silent   waiting
for the crackle of a train's sound
to form. I imagine the friction
transferring heat from the wheels
to the rails   to the dry fields.
Perhaps it distracts me from the creak
of a worn-down turbine vent
working to spin in the wind.

of Valley and Desert

{hear my name
as it should be}

i am the son of dona
i am the son of said

both run through me

        i throw rocks across water
        waiting for the swell
        to disrupt its pattern

        i rub the riverbank's deposits
        through the sweat pores
        of my linen flesh

        i dive without breath
        pull the thread of possession
        from its warpath

{hear my name
split like a river's veins}

i am of the san joaquin
i am of the nile

    i am of dona
    of her surface
    that buries marrow
    well under a requiem
    but can funnel a drift
    only if there are swans

                {hear my name
                cloak its homelands}

        i am of her san joaquin
        river and valley

                        i am of said
                        his voice raving
                        from the sediment
                        of a river's recession
                        because nothing regenerates
                        mortality like mourning

                {hear my name
                shoot from rupture}

        i am of his sahara
        i am of his nile

dona
said
san joaquin
nile
sahara

                {hear my name
                as it should be}

i am of dona and said
i am of valley and desert
i am of their water
i am of their dirt
all run through me
and i run through them

On Having Children

I could be the end of our bloodline
if it weren't for the allegories.

A patronymic transposes its succession
through all that is still unexplained.

> *Said*

Your picture is a screensaver for the tweed sport coat
I can smell the sand mat and marsh from.

You smoke a cigar on the Nile's promenade,
the Cairo tower's lattice frame a fragment
for the topography
ravaged by excavation.

You are aged as an apiary, brimming with combs
the honeybees hid from the new world
until you were ready.

> *Said*

> *Tamer Said*

You name me after the prophet's fruit.

The rendering of my name
is what fathers chew and line the gums
of their newborns with.

You ladle its nectar inside the pocket of a flatbread
spread like the balance between hope and fear.

I recite *Ayatul Kursi* quickly enough
to disguise my mistakes and rekindle the query
an oasis creates for the wayfarer.

>   *Said*

>   *Tamer Said*

>   *Said Tamer Said*

A new generation is generalized by the former.
The privilege of having children
is a lineage forged in suffering.

Our children are nomadic
before possessing their bodies. They will dance
when tomorrow becomes a retrospect of today.

You say fatherhood is an hourglass turned on its side.
I read you our poem   uncertain of where it begins.

Transformation

My three-year-old daughter cried
after I found her cat
dead behind the shed
in the wet heat
of an April afternoon.

Hundreds of maggots crawled
through the gash in its stomach,
feasted on the blood-soaked organs.
Squatting next to the gaseous flesh,
I chose not to dump the sack of soil
over the carcass.

Next week, the maggots will
leave a pile of bones,
grow wings and linger in circles
atop the rotten garbage can filled
with spoiled spaghetti, diapers,
and burger wrappers.

They will leave soon.
I don't count on them
stopping by for a meal,
buzzing above my head at 2 a.m.,
or flying through the wheat fields.

One day, when the maggots
swarm my rickety body and she has
children of her own,
she will understand why
I left her cat to rot.

II.

"Home is where you are appreciated, safe and protected, creative, and where you are loved – not where you are put in prison."

—from Nawal El Saadawi's interview with *The Guardian* (2015)

When Bone Thugs-n-Harmony Outshined Phil Collins on His Own Song

I am in my bedroom, ready for basketball practice
to siphon time by the milliseconds as if it's sacrificial
and I could only die
a hundred deaths at the hand of rehearsals
that cipher metamorphosis from the universe.
I worship this game
like it's time sensitive,
and the hardwood's sanctuary regurgitates
devotion
back to the saga of home.
I face the television's vessel,
draped in hand me down trousers
and a sleeveless jersey
smelling of laundry detergent from the mother
who washed them the year before,
and the mother before,
so that the dead of winter couldn't crack
the high school decal logo of a trojan warrior
taunting plumes of horsehair
through an imperial helmet's crest.
I post up the space heater like a defender,
dribble an invisible ball quick and methodical,
drop step and levitate,
contort my body mid-air
to melt the nylon ceiling to ores.
This testimony of beginnings
drips from a rim
in the land that labors over me.

The Mind is a Milk Curdle

The mind is a milk curdle when it becomes
overburdened. There is too much nature
to be contained in creation.

Your silhouette stoops through the wrinkles
of a woodshed, desperate to spare its timber
from the fire.

I muster the same disclaimer about memory
soothing my stomach's cloth with lather
and effervescence.

Return me to the clay
camouflaged by California poppies.

Return my marrow to the carbon it craves,
in as many lifetimes as grief will thaw
and replicate its nativity.

The land melts down to mudholes and lore.
Your cords are woven into a hammock
bracketing the chasms.

Neither my omission nor my closure
can pierce the periphery. The mind is drifting
to lift itself from the residuum.

Poem at Ten

—for my mother and after Sonia Sanchez

It is late, mid-July
in the valley's heat
sheathed in grooves.

I dribble a basketball
don't look down
at the earth
filming the leather.

I speak to god
for the first time
accepting
the threshold
of my marrow
that no one can tell me
about me
about entombing
the shrieks so deep
under the night
like a lost keepsake
twining my words
with the strain
of silk strings.

But you are here
near the end of a spiel
listening in the dark
on a webbed lawn chair
and heaven is somewhere
heavy under your soles.

Here is my spirit
turning back
to name the days
we'll leave behind.

The City

"A kind of map of the mind, or of life..."
—Alan Williamson

We always sought out our parents' attention
in the houses of our summers,
the hose water on hot asphalt driveways
shaded by tangled American flags.

They were the good old homes,
the backyards where we played quarters
to see whose knuckles would bleed the most,
and the public pools, jumping off diving boards
with open containers of red food dye
when the adults were around and watching.

There were the personal rites of passage:
walking the German Shepherds and black Labradors
to the wooded creeks that expunged funny
smoke odors and slapping sounds under the bridge,
running miles on the main street's dirt sidewalk
to the closest McDonald's for a strawberry shake.

The one rule was to be inside by the time
the first signs of night arrived
and we asked why the sun had to go down so fast,
pretended to understand the laws of physics and time
in the simple explanations whispered to us.

(One morning, a man clearing out road kill
found a boy's body in a drainage ditch
next to what was left of the raccoons and possums.

The boy's grip still cemented
on his bicycle hand bars.)

Under our forts composed of bed posts
and dark-shaded linens, we listened
to each other's horror fables in an attempt
to desperately prove how every single one of us
knew what danger was and how to conquer it.

It wasn't until later in our lives that we realized
at that age, we were no longer invincible
and learned all there was to know of independence.

McGaw Street

He wanted to go back out to the night,
feel the December draft through the bandage
wrapped around his forehead.

It was from the hole in the window,
the passenger's side that allowed the sharp air
to freeze our screams
inside the forest green Ford Taurus
and its outdated police package: broken antenna,
factory stereo missing the power button,
my wondering
how humans are really built for pressure.

He kept his head tilted back,
applied pressure to the metallic-tainted area
to stop the cloth seating from clotting the blood
that dripped past his shirt.

With the sight of each lamppost and crowding fog
we sped under, the neighborhood behind us
turned out of focus,
probably steam rising from the manholes.

It wasn't until he looked down at the dash,
couldn't see the airbag warning
through his composition
that he mumbled of heaven,
what he thought it would be like for the young.
Simple images: rivers, pearls, milk, and pomegranates.

He said he wasn't ready or was it worthy?
Said he preferred the hospital,

the path over the dry branches
winded in the potholes I knew how to avoid
and away from the glass shards in the street
that looked like ice crystals glowing in winter.

Post-mortem

He didn't smile in the picture upon arrival,
flannel shirt ruffled over the shoulders
brandishing abdominal abrasions.

X-rays caught the buckled knees
through the white body bag
masked on the dissection table.

The diener picked weed stems and seeds underneath
the nails, chopped off a long lock of brown hair,
windshield fragments stuck in the skin.

A body block lodged under the back
stretching the chest for the Y-incision.
Shears cracked the cavity, clammed-up organs
filled with rib bits.

Another incision from ear to ear,
tracing the crown covered in tire marks
from the pavement between Alpine and March
where the ambulance picked him up.

Arteries and ligaments detached, skin flaps
sewn back and the scalp tracked in Tacoma paint
restored to yesterday's ruins.

Eating a Peach on the Drive to Porterville

Some cities have a sign
announcing their achievements
only applicable to the valley:
the farming capital in Corcoran,
the harvest of raisins covered in plastic wrap
to protect from the thought of water in Selma,
the asparagus festival in Stockton,
where   before the recession,
you could win a free pound
by guessing how many sticks were in a bunch
without going over.
But the promised wages of generations
are buried beneath the dry land shadowed
in the deep rows of crops that seem endless
like the history of unionized hands
clinging to the memory
of pruning a hybrid fruit tree
at all the right spots
and just enough
to stimulate its growth.

I remember what Masumoto wrote
about being tied to a place during the time
of disasters, and when the juice is translucent,
running through the tunnels
of my beard until they wither,
I suction every bit of sustenance
stranded in the shallow canals of the pit.

"Slow down before you end up in the water like the rest of them!"

The pathogens have been passed down
from body to body
until we approach immunity,
my grandmother water skiing one legged
on the surface until the handle slips,
and she lets the waves carry her
as they lessen in height, lose power.

I tried floating to the observation station
fifty feet from shore and reached for the ladder,
but swam back to land in a fury
after being denied permission for my shortness.

I went in years later,
determined that my increased height
would make the feat possible,
but didn't take into consideration
that a recession was also synonymous
with a dried water level chart painted
in negative increments at the base of the station.

The waters are still muddy,
filled with crop runoff and salt intrusion
that the souls below, the ones who couldn't swim,
have lengthened their traces of preservation
hidden and suffocated under the shallow marsh.

Driving the road behind the water at night,
a teenager high on reefers and liquor
flips his vehicle over the dusk-chilled rocks,
splashes upside down.

In shock,
he forgets the seatbelt is locked in place,
and can't hold his head up long enough
to keep from filling with darkness.

Midnight in South Lake Tahoe

After the casinos
and the winning cash out slips
acting as coasters
for the free vodka drinks,
the hotel pillows harden
inside the lakefront
rental room illuminated
from the television.
Shows about killers,
their victims and methods,
hatched out plots and executions,
but mostly desires.
Outside, the waves haven't turned
to summer temperature yet
and their coldness coats
the sand
with each new current.

Somewhere near, a dog relieves itself,
turns to sniff the uncovered tracks,
and howls up for an owner.

Us in the kitchen, listening to Maxwell's "Pretty Wings"

Time will transform our omniscience
more than an afterlife.

Cucumber coriander and garlic
incubate inside a vinegar jar
like shapeshifters.

We censure their auras with small talk
and omens   juxtaposed

beneath the belly of a blade
grazing   the faithfulness
off each orgasmic knuckle.

One canister after another
is disinterred from its monument.

The heirlooms surrounding us
are an atonement for the orchids
plucked by a past life.

Replicate the pilgrimage again
and nothing can console our melancholy

of what fortune may come
but stay here   in this hiatus.
Perhaps the song will become the lexicon

of meaning sacrificed for rhythm
it hoped to escape   and we can dance

so effortlessly   under each other's arms
until the trumpets dwindle as they are.
Atop the compost   a strawberry pedicel

rewrites the metaphor in praise of
the breath and body we have left to offer.

Dameron Hospital, Stockton

The leaves from the willow oak
clog the sidewalk drain leading to the delta.
Cars sit there, collecting
pollen on their wiper blades.
This is the new expansion wing,
remodeled a decade ago on Acacia Street.
There must have been a new mother today
who trailed daffodil petals near the entrance.

When visiting your third-floor room,
I study the pierced peaks of the
EKG machine's communications.
Upon waking, you search the air
for your memory, and find it
in whichever visitor sits
at the open window lamenting
toward the cherry blossoms
and azaleas in the courtyard.
The volunteer who lost his wife here
serves coffee and attempts small talk
until your speech evaporates into sleep.

My conversation continues.
It's been hard to eat hasn't it?
I heard a preacher on tv
say our bodies create
two to three million new cells daily.
He didn't mention the kind
that you have in the stomach,
ones that are always hungry.
It's a little chilly in here, don't you think?

Here's an extra wool blanket
and a black beanie from mother,
your daughter.

The season is reverting back to Spring
and the cancer ward patients
secretly gather in the
designated smoking area.
I'm going to close this window, okay?
The second-hand stench
will climb the fire escape
and sift through the mesh screen.
I have to go home now and clean out
the closet of the clothes
you shrunk too small to wear.

Getting Dunked on by Jacki Gemelos

the last time i saw her /
we were in a north Stockton gym /
playing three on three /
it reeked of must and testosterone /
public enemy was bleeding between the planks /
the polish scuffed from all the sneakers /
i was standing in the short corner /
on defense /
clenching the hem of my tank top /
the ball swung from the high post/
she held it near the left wing /
jab- stepped her non-pivot foot in all directions/
then spun in reverse /
ran alongside the baseline /
as though leading an exodus /
through a map's repression /
i didn't even hear a dribble /
and slid over too late to stop /
by the time she jumped /
i started sinking /
into the creases like a dominion /
she hung on the rim with one hand /
that rim was a wreath /
streams woven with ivy /
the hardwood /
it pooled waves one after another /
to swallow the revelations /
only she would remember /
and i was just a detail /
trusting my defeat to the game /
without saying a word

Mourning Diana Solaegui in Solitude

Dear Diana.
Empress upon petals.
Your body recycled through the clay
in our wellspring of a city.
Forgive me for my indifference.
The psyche is a diaspore dispersed erratically.
Whirlwinds and tumble. What I would do
to detach its agony. Today,
I weave a crown from a tall weed of crabgrass,
and call monarchs to censure the rancor
in an ornament you would remember.
The cortege ends with an undying godliness
of where the migration originates.
An open mic sign-up sheet binds to a billboard
in the remnants of a corner cafe
traumatized by mnemonics for every ambition
forsaken in its wake.
I am present, later than I should be,
but here.   Dear Diana.
Mantras. Apologies. Motifs.
Thank you for the love my friend.

Elegies for the Central Valley

I.

I remember the moment
of re-entering the valley
by the feel of the temperature
in the air layering
the skin on my hand
with warmth and crop dust,
a signal of welcoming.

I looked at the lights
on the horizon,
thought they were little
open fires
needing water,
but they were from the homes
of a development,
and I saw the sound towers,
the highest marks in the land,
blinking blue and red
in alternation.

II.

A store-owner tells a joke
of having an extra supply of plywood
in the back
that he could nail
over the windows
for when the graveyard
adds another plot.

Someone washes a car,
refusing wishful thinking
that rain will come
clear the smudges
and dead insect streaks.

The johns pass the dining hall
next to tent city
for a girl who hasn't been able
to smell past the zone
of slick latex and recyclables.
She is virtuous.

III.

Before we knew how to garden
we believed in farms
and markets,
a seeded watermelon
and a batch of chopped chestnut.

My father and I sold tomatoes
in the summer
out of his pickup bed
to restaurants along Highway 12
and Grant Line Road,
"escape routes"
they were referred to as,
by those who had intentions
of remaining,
but wanted the allure
of something greater.

IV.

Our family would eat fried chicken
and corn on a public table
facing the delta,
trying to see who would be the first
to spot a steelhead trout elevate,
break the rhythm of the tide
for a moment,
and absorb the heat
that gathers above the surface.

V.

Somewhere under Whistler Street
is a place I sprained my wrist
bicycling down a hill
too fast and flipping
over the handlebars.
My mother was grateful for the dirt,
noticing the sticks in the ground
with flags and measurements.
She said someday, this will be
a hard road,
someday soon,
we will have to find
another open space
to walk after dinner.

VI.

Neighborhood hero
(hit by a truck on Interstate 5)
couldn't cross the Calaveras

unless backtracking
six miles by foot.

The old sounds barriers
crumble for construction,
a new Fastlane
paved over the spray-painted
spot of death.

His initials scratched with
a pocketknife
on a park bench
around the corner from home.

They buried him
Islamically
in a clean shroud without a coffin
and everyone took turns
shoveling their share of dirt.

VII.

Refinished furniture
sits in an open garage,
attracting a slight breeze
straining through the cattails,
and their flat blade leaves.

It waits for dryness,
for an owner to reach some
sort of perfection
by sanding away
all the impurities that remain.

A can of golden oak gloss stain
sits open nearby on a shelf,
a bristle brush handle sticking out,
and a thawed oxygen mask.

I Lip-synced Ready for the World Instead of Pushing Carts for Target

After a supervisor said I wasn't allowed
to wear headphones while on-duty
I insulated myself in a car
near the lot's exit way
restrained into the passenger seat's fabric
and said   you will not find me
or my red shirt from there.
Reclining back as far as weight would tolerate
I watched the customers wander in all directions
and began to pull artificial high notes
from my diaphragm   for no reason
but to deviate conjunctions to the future.
By the guitar solo
I was halfway through a menthol
constricting its smoke
to reach my channels
and the cords
loosened from the trunk's subwoofers
repeating after each other
a C   into a D
the customers looking into that space
of air tracing an E-minor
with my fingers and a cigarette butt.
The drums amplified after,
arguing against the world's grandeur
trickling down to a dreamland
where a generation's precursors
translate   compositions from prayer
and I slapped the steering wheel
like it was a sheet of stretched parchment
embalmed on a mantle.

I knew it was ending
when the supervisor tapped her knuckles on the glass
to make me forget what it meant to be lost
in the midst of worlds reciprocating
their gravity   atop my tracks and divots.
I thought to get out and return to work
but stared at the barrier separating us
as the rhapsody withheld inside
dimmed the window to dawn.

In Defense of *Queef*

a heat wave   voyaging the valley's vignette
embeds my flesh
a salvation   as intricate as seasons
lasting as long as each other

there were once   water towers
near the interstate
reckoning the tules   from the city's stupor
so the marsh could become
subtle and fluid

you lean on my pillars
like a clothesline tempts the landscape
with moisture   and shadows

i hear a soliloquy   performed
for more than just me
and think of   the night i tried
     floating in a slough
wrinkled like russet linens

the diablo range   was to the west   losing
its ridges and peaks   through the altitude

i was accompanied   by a yield of wheat grains
beneath a bascule bridge   lifting both leaves
in a humid unison

the temperature   withdrew its gauntness
     pulled its delta
closer to the Pacific's   tremble

and i tell you   that your air   is endless

like a willow's mural   running its breath
to the end of summer

Brookside Park Blacktop

He finds his spot feet behind
the three-point line
on a section of asphalt
that sinks deeper
than any other part of the court.

His defenders, thinking the shot
impossible,
stay near the key,
hands interlocked atop their heads,
catching their breath.

Licking his off-hand index finger,
he sticks it to the sky,
gauging the direction of the wind.
That's an airball someone exhales—
and he shoots, releasing
the ball from his chest,
holding three fingers up high
as he waits for the chains to rise
and sink in one drift.

A Robin Stopped by This Morning

A robin stopped by this morning
when the kitchen window was written
with finger-tipped initials and tracings
of skin oil the air tried to withhold.

I was measuring fennel and fenugreek
by the pinch, adding cumin, coriander,
black peppercorns and cloves
into a stainless-steel skillet.

The robin flexed its claws, wrapped them
around the dogear's curve of redwood fence,
reminding me to also break
a star anise pod and cinnamon stick in half.

I warmed the spices over medium-high heat,
stirring a porcelain spoon
from the bottom, until the flavors trickled
out of their cocoons, circled the room.

The robin hopped onto the window-sill
to follow each scoop of spice flooding
an old coffee grinder ingrained with shadows
of the *masala* that came earlier.

I could only grind in short batches,
the rhythm of wanting interrupted,
the aromas lingering in their steam,
sifting through one another.

The robin raised its chest feathers
for me to compare the color of redness

to the amount of turmeric
I folded into the *masala's* conglomerate.

It was cold, but I held your body
like the soundwaves of language,
dispersed to understanding.

The robin dabbed its bill to the glass,
the *masala* a memory of migration
asking *when will you visit again?*

In South Sacramento

—after James Wright

The remnants of a ripened lemon tree
interrupt
a concrete laden driveway
near Hollyhurst

the trunk   severed in its center
down an angle.

A single fruit   cascading from the gut   splits juice
on the pavement.
I climb the canopy's chimera how I am meant to.

The teeth of a crosscut saw are like kinetic mirrors
invoking momentum from the backbones

they capture. The bottom branches sweep the leaves
off their pedestals.

The Valley, as Told from a Pet Hospital Parking Lot

Bermuda grass on leaves.
Crickets ricochet desires to the abruptness of dusk.
The masks we wear
are too large to contain life close to us.
Our dog is inside
purging red grapes from his stomach
that he scoured the couch's underbelly for.
Sitting on the curb
my legs straddling a drainage grate
supplementing the delta with rainwater.
An interstate splits the eldest neighborhoods
into demography and flaws.
We separate from other people
by the length

        two paces

        two strides

        two seams

of an emblem
can betray the breadth before us.
The calmness of a mulberry
lurching its branches is enough
to stimulate the dreams
we withhold from ourselves.

Shapes are real as the dirt
curdled around our outsoles
overcome by praxis.
Symbols are figments
speaking through us in tongues
until mouths turn numb.
By midnight, our dog is released
with a drawstring leash fatiguing his neck
and half a grape left to navigate
its escape to the valley's blindfold
the only touch we can forgive.

stockton

*"some rivers flow back
toward the beginning
i never learned to swim"*
—Lucille Clifton

i was born
in a northern valley
of california

c is for current

there are more i's
in california
than i have
siblings

the deltas undertones
stir a shirt to the surface
near the banks
a bucket of quick dry cement
waits
for its possessor

why am i here

the top of stockton
floats into the drought
of dry crinkled vines
the wine is a sharp white

they are still here
lurking in the cattails

    captain weber

    commodore stockton

  the city's name irks the natives

    mayor podesto

      weber

      stockton

      podesto

my mother had a child
that drowned before birth

when the rain does come

the ground has been too dry
to absorb the water

who can swim
when the tides
of the city

reach the tides
of the delta

will i sink
in this stockton
on the inland delta

which way

will the water

drag our bodies

why do we

ask questions

Kayaking off Brannan Island

This afternoon   a Sandhill Crane untangles cattails
with its bill   churning the wetland's surface
to primordial bronze and bones.
Both rivers converge
overcome the inferno opening portals   unprovoked
for a purge of reckoning.

A Brown Pelican's wingspan shelters the bottleneck
we paddle through   the current working against us
vagabonds   liberated from the façade. How
fatiguing and gelatinous it once felt.

This evening   voids are immolated into morning
so then   we can fathom our nirvana
without fearing tomorrow.

After I Returned

After I returned,
an empty well bucket hung from a rope
the windlass wanting to click,

sulfur and calcium crystals
tapping against the cylinder's wooden planks.

I found a bullet shell in the gutter
before it was carried to the storm drain,
and pinched it to study the grooves,
asking if it belonged
to someone I knew.

The heat traversed the limits
beyond my hand.
I threw the shell
the way one tries to skip a flat rock
over a calm river,
and then accepted the futility
of excavating.

To the Passerby

Across town, far from the hot tar dropping
towards Little Manila, shallow lake tides
soften and soak the dock's wooden planks
the pintails use to line in regularity
like the first wave of soldiers in battle.

The blue-gray bill expelling the inedible
in each mouthful
and I awoke under the agricultural patterns
of their flights,
fearing an impending migration,
then released whatever life I had left.

I knew the stay would be short,
as if the next destination
promised to provide better sustenance and safety
enveloped in the flounces of a swift softness.

Remember the scent of sprouting asparagus crowns
through the cow manure and drying delta water,
the truth of our city, its origins and intentions.

III.

"voyage, oh voyage!
the final fire that ravages the air
unveils the soil on which
we walk aimlessly
and tirelessly

the hypocrisy of the strong protects us
from home…"

"if we write, it's that we can't
sing, if we sleep, it's that we
can't live

memory is good for nothing
most of the time…"

—from Etel Adnan's *Time*

"Days of Our Livez" is a better Bone Thugs-n-Harmony song than "Tha Crossroads"

—ending with lines from Fatimah Asghar

It begins
with history
backtracked
to its predecessors
hoarding piano cords at their intervals until they bleed
like intermediaries.
Listen for the samples
being revived from their grief in order to become
relevant again,
retelling the stories not surrendered
to complacency.
When the lyrics come later
incandescent candles
are burning behind glass   more than I dare
to count   and the memorials
bear witness
to the land's pseudonyms
I mumbled in baritone
so long ago.
The rhyme schemes become more abrupt
as the song continues.
They murder the recurrences
that cannot be rebirthed   into this phenomenon
where *my love for the past is like my love / for most things
I only feel it when / I leave.*

Failed Migration to Egypt, 2007

I remember what I choose to   of sand
the threads of your hair unfurling
over a stallion's withers,
striding into Giza's restriction,
the province of Khafre's pyramid.
It fulfilled us to berate the guards
like superiors, kick color on their slacks
for our quest to recover ourselves.

I remember what I choose to   of water
the streaming accent of a rip current
restoring the vacuum of your wet wrist
dipped into the Nile's compress
from the side of our felucca.
We each propelled an oar
with the skyline of Cairo before us
performing the lyric of its history.

I remember what I choose to   of warmth
the new coals coating the aluminum
over the bowled clay head of an *argeela*,
the ice churning to an idle thaw
against the glass base. I asked to share
the apple tobacco with you, become awakened
in a breach of arrhythmia, but the fumes
hung suspended and sour with pause.

I remember what I choose to   of breath
like a contranym prefacing context.
A binary, you whispering a goodbye
with an ersatz dialect of Arabic
against the desert's gasp of pull,

toting my being to its truth entombed
in a sarcophagus marked by myth
and the distant hallucination of you.

from trilateral roots

—after Craig Santos Perez

[ra-ha-meem   (womb):]
i named my first star   on a farmhouse roof
    in *Kafr El Zayat*   flooding fennel seed
      into the divots of a mortar
      an oud's fifth string
danced like a caudex

[rahma   (compassion):] the moon blued its
dust to our voices
a mother tongue unadulterated   a *nasheed*
    of desert roses surrendering
      to their stems

[Ar-Rahman   (The Most Compassionate):]
i lifted a sleeping mat   filled with plump palm fibers
              away from the fire's timbre
        to pray along the earth's outgrowth
with the words   of a second language
    milking my bones

        [raheem   (merciful):] a relative
   turned my body
by her henna tresses   a bridge of kinship
             unrolling my shoulders
        to hear the grazing of ghosts
          in the pastures below
and the star's name
      was a metonym
    for her   who I cannot save

My Grandmother Would Have Loved Chick-fil-A

Not just for the food but because they're closed on Sundays & Sundays are for nostalgia & I feel bad that she settled for Wendy's all those years when she could have enjoyed biscuits   waffle-fries   & an owner glorifying god quicker than he can pressure fry chicken & They say Truett Cathy was a faithful steward to the end & and he was born in 1921   months before her & we all make our choices but what an opportunity missed & today is the first day of E'id 2017
the holiday after Ramadan's hunger is quenched & my grandmother lies in bed   drenched in the dearth of mortem & she is holding her Jesus somewhere disclosing the antitheses that tried to deceive her   the ones she withstood   *so where is my kingdom* she asks & over the next two days of E'id   I help clean out her apartment & stop counting at 16 bibles   some on nightstands ladled in yellow Wendy's napkins & I remember the only time I went to church as a child & the adults made us race against each other in a circle outlined in chalk on the blacktop like a hypnotic spiral & they kept howling   *Jesus Saves   Jesus Saves
         Jesus Saves* & we converged in the middle of this circle true to the galaxies we were & in the middle of this circle was a stuffed animal for every chase & each child who didn't win had to go again until they could hold up their animals like war spoils   but   I   was chubby   & I was slow   & Jesus couldn't save the surges of baby weight suffocating my lungs & Jesus couldn't save me from being the last one left without a stuffed animal & they made me run again and against myself until their faces salted the night like the stars on our flag & different colored plush hung from their

fingers like marionettes & when I collapsed in the middle of their circle clasping a synthetic lion they broke out in song *I am a C*   *I am a C-H* *I am a C-H-R-I-S-T-I-A-N*   *YEE-HAW*   & I left church more Muslim than I'll ever be & my grandmother still loves her blood & curses my pick for god

but how is it that she hated Islam & died on a Muslim holiday & I'm the first to her grave before the wake & I'm the last to tell her story   minus my damnations & it's better than all the other stories & after the wake I take chicken from the chafer grill & heap it on my plate piece by piece like shrine stones & I hide behind this edifice of chicken swamped in blind spots
         not believing this is as good as it could be & then I start eating

To Make Love in a Hearse

First, stretch out the drapes
and vacuum them well
to help absorb some of the steam
between you and the windows.

Place blankets over the framed
platform for comfort
or go bare-wooded
so sweat can act as an adhesive
to whoever is on bottom.

If the springs and rollers are too
squeaky or dry, spray some WD-40
to get them moving
and grip the bier pin plates
for better leverage.

If not in a lying position,
keep a hunched back and watch
for your head on the dome lighting.

There should be plenty of space,
unless of course, there's a casket.
And if that's the case,
improvise.

The Origin of Fear

The first time I shot a gun,
I was on a dark levee
above a receding creek,
fidgeting with the safety guard,
aiming towards an inclined slope.

After the chamber's fireball
singed the hair off my hand,
I ran, not thinking about the bullet's
terminal velocity and descent.

Years later, a friend's father
was driving for groceries
when a small circle of light
radiated a direct line from the windshield
to the passenger's headrest.

Around the same time, a 15-year-old child
sitting in a bedroom, hears a cluster of shots,
falls to the floor below the life goals
written on the walls,
feeling the pool of blood
encapsulate his head.

Today, I browse the internet,
filtering through victims of unsolved shootings
dating back so many years,
trying to believe that all of my lead tips
died at the end of their flights,
and fell into an empty field
or a cool body of water.

I Haven't Been Keeping Up on Pluto Much These Days

—at the El Dorado County Community Observatory

It happens that looking directly
through a reflector becomes a tragedy
once the constellations are unsettled on a night
the air is fresh with pine heaped from the foothills.
We praise the light years in the back of a sky theater
with our heads resting on concrete
while the guides speak of the millennia to come.
They say the earth is like a spinning top
maintaining its momentum, only for so long
before it forfeits inertia and recalibrates direction
to another distance.
I commemorate a moment in Mexico weeks earlier
when I felt the axis wobble
like a little jolt peeled the atmosphere from its reel
and suspended the tides too reluctant
to pull the land's threads
under their revolving onyx.
Everything is nothing, but cyclical.
I admit then, it is not new for me to hear them say
Pluto is now a dwarf planet in the metaphor
of star fields, rewriting itself to keep us guessing
what variant will arrive next.
But we can look at Saturn's rings in the meantime
tug their particles into submission
and Jupiter's *Europa* and *Ganymede*
overlapping the other's mirage
above the elevation's forgiveness.
All we're left to wonder is *Andromeda*
as ominous as the city's penumbra below

bulging from the farmland.
Such mercilessness rousing our memories
to ignore the gravity.

Existential Crisis through the Windstorm, in a Humboldt County Yurt

"This is the riddle that drives the mind crazy: that the opener and what is opened are the same!"
— Rumi

Daybreak counts its hours backwards. The nebula
is indifferent to the present

emptiness. The Pacific exerts a spur of appetite
behind us. Nothing is boundless.

Everything invisible to the canvas's makeshift vessel
forges joists and girders

out of redwood. Farther in elevation, a herding trail
revolves near an overhang.

Each interpretation is contingent upon how many
yellow, albino trees

outlive the ghosts of the forest. A void could often be
understood by the paradox

developing from the vestige. We must lock ourselves
inside the riddle that Winter

is nothing more than burlap plucked from Spring.

The Poet's Partner Karaokes "Rainbow" by Kesha

The lyric guide conceals each passing word through the television's veil whether they are sung or not. They fall into an epitome of kaleidoscopes while the voices in the poet's head are terrified of teleporting somewhere original.

The song's trance attempts to outlast the suffering. The poet has become a recluse in his partner's subconscious where he wades on a submerged harbor deck during a downpour over the mainland. His partner pulls away in a canoe, steering towards open water. The poet knows the sea is full of too many pinnacles to silence its prostration, and gives in to the gathering.

His partner pulls the song's climax from her spectrum like a piece of higher land rejuvenating the poet. She paints the undertones into a symmetry of reservoirs and potions. The poet transcends back to the room's acoustics resurrecting the final chorus atop an orchestra of artifacts. His partner commands the ending to declare her tears from the noise. The poet blends the indigo into a new sequence, and calls out for more rain.

Ascent

In this visit
to the graveyard
I see that beneath the headstone
is a ditch
and in that ditch
is a box
and in that box
is a body
and in that body
there was a soul
a soul a body a box a ditch and
myself
alone beneath a headstone.

Inauguration Day, 2017

The wake was quick,
spectators bemoaning
over the synthetic body,
probing its soil
as if an apocalyptic relic
stowing a copper crown,
a *tabula ansata*
stigmatized in censure.

We consume dinner rations
with dullness,
finely sharpening idioms
of a mended memoir,
its author the remonstration
of occupants
coiled in a concocted
reconstruction of records.

Consumed in a residual
strategic transition,
our backs are turned
to the embodiment
unfolding out of itself
like the creases of a flag
shrieking in the wind,
its disputed truth resurrected.

I Must Have Been Beautiful *aka Shyla Styles Has Died*

Shyla Styles has died. I can't help but wish myself
dead too. It's hard to stop fantasizing her flesh,
oiled and contorted in a sticky fluid
waterlogged by blossoms, it would drown demons,
sacrifice itself like the symmetry of stars
until desiccated, and thirsting to be still.

Shyla Styles has died and I mourn the loss of stills
that titillated me to imagine myself
as true to the prayers my father hawked at the stars
and sealed magazines beneath my bed, of flesh
poked with freakish cocks I thought were demons
when they flared up, withered from their own fluid.

Shyla Styles has died. I freestyled in the fluids
of innocence split like water, because I still
wanted the buffering scenes from a screen's demon
to reproduce the sweeping fragments of myself
on top her body, as if I could press her flesh
clear through mine, reach for an annex behind stars.

Shyla Styles has died, and she was never my star.
She was not my glassblower, crooning through fluids
to then suffocate in disquiet, so her flesh
could be a chimera of *American* stills.
I see their outskirts cutting a looking-glass self
at the pleats, shoveling shallow holes for demons.

Shyla Styles has died, and I will be your demon.
I will be your monster for praising a porn star,
but how much more do you think I can hate myself

for being a sleepless child, cinched in fluids
of a nameless man and upstairs room that is still
undressing and marveling my vessel of flesh?

Shyla Styles has died. I've known to shame my flesh
since then, like chasing a fix in needled demons
that can poach a spirit from a porcelain still
faster than a blackout swaddling phosphorous stars.
I suppose we each have a story that's fluid,
moist with mystery, springing from itself.

Shyla Styles has died, still and sprawled out like a star,
her flesh swallowing all the embalming fluid,
and no one knows why I save the demons for myself.

The Sunflower

—after Taha Muhammad Ali

It was nightfall
when I chopped you down
with a cheap machete
and stroked its edge
through the wool
of your shoots.
You were by the delta,
staring into the water,
unstirred and curtained
like molasses.
I burned your florets
inside a mason jar
until the disc bled fumes
to wrinkles, and you
rapped your psyche
to the glass.
What did I lose
by unearthing the truth
that you are not mine
to occupy,
that I cannot resent
the world like a Bedouin
shouting to the shores
that fostered him?
What can suspend time,
disrupt a sweep hand
spellbound to amnesia
so that a falcon
can still be a falcon
released to the celestial?

What will happen
when I return to the sanctuary,
to the soil I stole you from,
its bearings buried by rhytides?
What will happen now,
that I lift the lid
and leave you to the sun?

All I Know Is How to Stop Breathing

A bound bookmark tassel is gagged
and burned somewhere in the preface,
processions hang from an overhead conveyer belt
circling inside a chicken slaughter plant.

I am sick with this infection,
climbing a fermented hierarchy
of feverish speech pacified by elixirs,
restrained by leather-strapped hallucinogens.

The medicine was elsewhere, in *'asal,*
our foraged, restorative nectar
coaxed within the comb's thickness,
to be lynched off the inquisitor's precipice.

A decrowed cockerel trickles saliva,
disoriented in an artificial dusk
under the executioner's sharpened carbon,
mouthing its riot to the keeper.

Listening to *Man on the Moon: The End of Day*

The sky falls for an algorithm:

a Ziplock's crystal contents
cherry-picking the air
from every throat,
illuminating them with a paralysis
that leaps between our teeth.

There is no lesson
on transcending euphoria,
gnawing the jaw to a wattle
of silver linings,
fiending for the rebirth.

Our childhoods looped
into swift afterglow
like ghosted contours.

It is a dry night in November.

One of our own
straggles an interstate shoulder
by the fugue of his gingham
and when the tremor strikes,
a whiskey fume climbs sound walls
as far as time will lift,
before the river below
inhales and paints it to the columns.

Another witness is unearthed.

The stillness
shrouds his body like a lion mane
for where there are no dreams.

We pray straight as a comb's teeth
to go higher   and higher
so that we *could see the universe*
and forget our way home.

Fatima's Martyrdom

—after *Fatima's Coochee-Coochee Dance* (1896)

Her image will not dissolve
under the strangulation
of censor bars
blanking her *bedlah*
careening
only to her rhythm,
a golden gardenia absorbed
through a slit of custody.
She has been profiled
in silent footage,
distributed as an exotic
beacon of the east,
replicated in folklore.
Inside a Moroccan restaurant,
I scan a hanging collection of sequins
and beaded fringes
sewn to a bolero shrug
for the faces that followed,
their projections pressed
into a collection
of calculated labels.
My abstracted face
becomes concentrated
in an audible reflection.
I hear the thudding
of a *darbuka*,
the rich ululation
reviving the seams
of consciousness.

And we look up at her,
twirling her wrists
as if imprisoned in nostalgia,
dying for us to be seen.

Nabra's Moon

—for Nabra Hassanen

It comes new, clear as the cymbal
sculpted from alloy,
and the locusts are tree-bound,
bouncing between ivy and honeysuckle
so eternity can migrate like pendulums,
quench the womb of its hunger.

I ask America
why the water here is waxed
and the roots weeping in a labyrinth
that feeds off the mirage of crescents.

> *O' America. Where are the harvests*
> *you've crowned? Where are the ghosts*
> *relinquishing their skin to water?*

History is often synthesized
to be a quiet chandelier,
a light erecting statues and fountains
for the spectacle of memorial.
But there is still fire, the kind
that splits land
even quarter-moons will drop their plasma
to melt the embers.

There was her body here,
face-down
floating
like a mooring buoy   tethered in chain link
and the soul was a boulder

embedded on shore
watching the retrieval.

How is she remembered?
A short hashtag before a name
made of ash and waning
the wind can't keep trending
beyond the olive trees?

This pond belongs to her now,
this is her body of water,
and America is shaming the way a *hijaab*
wraps pinnacles around the young.

> *O' America. Does this mean I can blame you*
> *for creating baseball and its composite bats*
> *with sweet spots that spew sensation to wounds?*

This is her moon,
silhouetted with lilacs
to drag rapture through madness
one bough at a time.
It signals prayer.
It segregates the soul from body
like a drum carder.

It pulls her name out of the water.

Where Will I Find *America?*

—for Deah, Yusor, & Razan, ending with lines from
Mahmoud Darwish

Where will I find America? A swollen graveyard
of shunned Carolina clay incites its crevice,
consents a repetition of impresses to the lamenting,
as if tapping wooden spiles into a sugar maple.
Their recitations will swing like a severed hinge
to summon covenant verses for your space
median   withheld   to steal beginnings
from contempt and the breadth of othering.
There have been martyrs before,
a cinder's desire flushed in a bedrock
where belonging is sung through shrapnel, a ballad
weaving the dankness of an orifice
like kindled frankincense.
They will receive you across partitions
as lost relatives reframing a past rift,
as elders tracing a journey with cotton threads
and mantras for those that come after
I am
from
here
and here
is here
and I
am I
and here
I am
and I
am here.

Reclamation

This flag is an amalgamation of feelings
purified in kerosene as it should be.
America's cavities erupt into the pretense
plagiarized from its own parables.
2.23 miles is a disclaimer unbeknownst
to the odyssey blind spots burden themselves with,
to bear depressions and tread marks
down to their core.
The gateway to Appalachia and mayhem
is ablaze. Praise the mountaintop
that cannot be undone by man,
nor his weaponry. 8 shells. 8 voids. 8 tunnels
to an intercession looming in the wind.
Officers in Minnesota's fable
shrink a kingship of oceans down
to a waterless canal disquieting cycles
in the vain of all that is political.
A hashtag appropriates namesakes
out of timelines American as crimson.

> Ahmaud Arbery
> Breonna Taylor
> George Floyd

Prayers recited synchronically.
Pedestals to be prostrated upon.
Rinse and repeat.
All of us or none.
Fuck the blue and red of America.
Fuck the de facto that is American white.
Fuck the folklore of law
metastasizing in the name of America.

How do our proverbs sound now?
Flame be to this listless flag,
indignant as its justice.
Our America.
Sophistic. Fallacy. Subconscious.
Smoke and millstones.
Ever more our country.

Acknowledgements

Thank you to the following journals for publishing earlier versions of poems appearing in this book:

Carcinogenic Poetry: "stockton"

City of Davis Arts & Cultural Affairs Poem of the Month: "of Valley and Desert"

Clade Song: "Eating a Peach on the Drive to Porterville" and "Elegies for the Central Valley"

Confrontation: "Lamb Slaughter"

Curator Magazine: "the coming fire"

Dissident Voice: "Composition" and "Nabra's Moon"

FreezeRay Poetry: "The Night Bone Thugs-n-Harmony Reunited" and "My Grandmother Would Have Loved Chick-fil-A"

From Sac: "The City," "After I Returned," and "Midnight in South Lake Tahoe"

Full of Crow: "A Panegyric for a Self, Hidden Within" and "Inauguration Day, 2017"

Futures Trading: "A Childhood Around 1999" and "To Make Love in a Hearse"

Glass: A Journal of Poetry: "I Haven't Been Keeping Up on Pluto Much These Days"

Heavy Feather Review: "*from* **trilateral roots**"

Hobart: "Poem at Ten"

Literary Orphans: "2011: On the Metro to Tahrir"

Matter Monthly: "Where Will I Find *America?*"

Mobius: The Journal of Social Change: "The Origin of Fear"

Occupy Poetry: "Rite of Passage"

Phantom Kangaroo: "Ascent"

The Rag: "Transformation"

Triggerfish Critical Review: "Tweaking," "Slow down before you end up in the water like the rest of them!," "Brookside Park Blacktop," "Dameron Hospital, Stockton," and "Shame"

Tule Review: "There is No Blood"

Writing Disorder: "Letter to Lucy Corin"

Zone 3 Press: "Failed Migration to Egypt, 2007" and "Fatima's Martyrdom"

The following poems also appeared in the *Monday Night Press* chapbook *Which Way Will the Water Drag Our Bodies?*: "The City," "A Childhood Around 1999," "There is No Blood," "The Sunflower," "Eating a Peach on the Drive to Porterville," "Elegies for the

Central Valley," "The Origin of Fear," "Dameron Hospital, Stockton," "Brookside Park Blacktop," "Ascent," "Tweaking," "Slow down before you end up in the water like the rest of them!," "All I Know is How to Stop Breathing," "the coming fire," "To Make Love in a Hearse," "I Must Have Been Beautiful," and "stockton"

ن – و – ر

"The Night Bone Thugs-n-Harmony Reunited" was inspired by Hanif Abdurraqib's "The Summer A Tribe Called Quest Broke Up"

"Lamb Slaughter" was inspired by Joshua McKinney's "Chicken Slaughter"

"Poem at Ten" was inspired by Sonia Sanchez's "A Poem for My Father"

"The City" was inspired by Alan Williamson's "A Map of Life"

"Dameron Hospital, Stockton" was inspired by Mary Oliver's "University Hospital, Boston"

"Mourning Diana Solaegui in Solitude" was inspired by Juan Felipe Herrera's "Ode to José Montoya"

"In South Sacramento" was inspired by James Wright's "In Ohio"

"stockton" was inspired by Lucille Clifton's "memphis"

"Dayz of Our Lives" is a better Bone Thugs-n-Harmony song than "Tha Crossroads" was inspired by, and borrows lines from Fatimah Asghar's "My Love for Nature"

"*from* **trilateral roots**" was inspired by Craig Santos Perez's "*from* **aerial roots**"

"My Grandmother Would Have Loved Chick-fil-A" was inspired by Hanif Andurraqib's "The Year My Brother Stopped Listening to Hip-Hop"

"Existential Crisis through the Windstorm, in a Humboldt County Yurt" was inspired by, and borrows lines from Jalaluddin Rumi's "Die Before You Die"

"Ascent" was inspired by Lucille Clifton's "testament"

"The Sunflower" was inspired by Taha Muhammad Ali's "The Falcon"

"Where Will I Find *America?*" was inspired by, and borrows lines from Mahmoud Darwish's "Take Care of the Stags, Father"

ذ – ك – ر

All praise and glory be to Allah for the daily gifts, blessings, and privileges granted to me. Thank you to my parents Dona and Said, my brother Sharif, my maternal grandparents Juanita and Harold, my paternal grandparents Tahani and Badawi, and the countless relatives who spanned continents to help make my journey possible.

Sincerest gratitude to the mentors, friends, collaborators, etc. for their support and wisdom: Coach Tom Galvin, Dr. David "Rock" Nylund, Dr. Krishna Guadalupe, Diana Solaegui, Joshua Clover, Joe Wenderoth, Rhony Bhopla (ShiluS Publications), James Lee Jobe, Syd Castain, Christina Magaña, Geoffrey McCain, Sparkle Crenshaw, Kerri Schofield, Ayotunde Khyree Ikuku II, Jason Bayani, Eliud "Julio" Cruz, Jessica Wickens, and Mohammed Naseem Barase.

So much love goes out to Bone Thugs-N-Harmony whose music has guided me to faith, family, and poetry since I was 13-years-old. Thank you for inspiring me to dream, for being the shoulder I can lean on.

I would like to acknowledge the Northern Valley Yokuts and the Plains Miwok as the Indigenous custodians of this land now referred to as Stockton, this land I am privileged to call home.

For Erika Angini Prasad (Erika beautiful). Language is too limiting most of the time. Words can never encompass the love my soul feels for you, and from you. I cherish you as the creative, intellectual, powerful Queen that you always are. Thank you for believing in the best version of me, for being my BFF-FFFFFF. I love you eternally.

About the Author

Tamer Said Mostafa (pronouns: he/him/his) is a poet and writer from Stockton, California. He is a graduate of the Creative Writing program at University of California, Davis This is his first full-length collection of poetry. He can be reached on the following platforms:

https://www.facebook.com/ttymehendo

https://twitter.com/ttymehendo

https://www.instagram.com/ttymehendo

www.ingramcontent.com/pod-product-compliance
Lightning Source LLC
LaVergne TN
LVHW041630070426
835507LV00008B/540